Preface

It's amazing to me that after spending more than ten years in the design field, I still get to have firsts. Last year I opened my very first boutique, Rummage, in LA's design district. Running it brings me back to my roots. As a kid growing up in Cerritos, California, I haunted flea markets and thrift shops and yard sales, always looking for interesting things to bring home. Although my parents didn't appreciate my junking, my flair for design started to gain recognition by the time I was a teen. My eclectic bedroom even landed on the cover of a section of the local paper about cool teen rooms.

It took quite a few years for me to realize that I could make a living doing what came so naturally to me. But in my work today, I use those same strategies, seeking out diamonds in the rough for my clients: a sofa with great bones or a unique lamp that simply needs a new shade. I like to think my greatest talent lies in seeing the potential in art, furniture—even people. And now with Rummage, I get to bring all my favorite things together in one place and showcase my own custom pieces. You'll find the mix of high and low that's the epitome of my design sensibility.

Which brings me here, to my very first book. Looking through photos of past projects, I was able to break down the ideas and processes that make up my aesthetic. Each chapter focuses on a different element that's essential to good design. To me, there are no hard-and-fast rules. It all boils down to knowing who you are and what you like and trusting your instincts. But a little guidance can't hurt, and that's where this book comes in. My hope is that it will help you create a home that makes you happy every time you walk in the door. Enjoy.

KISHANI PERERA
Los Angeles, 2011

OPPOSITE: My shop, Rummage, is like my second home. Every item in the store expresses my sensibility, from the custom furniture of my own design to the reimagined vintage finds and ethnic pieces. And the displays, which feature a vintage dress form turned floor lamp, life-size faux trees, and colorful butterflies, show my whimsical side.

Introduction

by Molly Sims

I'm an actress, so I know I can be dramatic. But I truly believe that to design is to experience life and all of life's emotions. It's creative and controlled, messy and precise, passionate and analytical, daunting and rewarding, obscure and revelatory. And I love it. I had just moved from New York to Los Angeles for work. I was on set five days a week and working seven. And I had made my very first design mistake. Knowing I couldn't do it all myself, I hired a designer with fantastic ideas but, as I came to learn, zero follow-through. Months after our agreed-upon deadline, little had been done, and I had no time to finish—I was a wreck.

Enter Kishani, bless her soul. Hollywood Hills, we have liftoff! Under her watchful eye, the kitchen cabinets were stripped and repainted, marble countertops imagined and installed, tile floors swiftly refinished, pillows tossed, paintings hung, vintage pieces restored, and lighting electrified. Kishani not only had a great eye, but she also had the ability to get the job done and work within my budget.

I was living in LA but continued to work from time to time in Manhattan, and I realized I needed a base there. I found a contemporary one-bedroom on the edge of Soho; it had great bones, was very open, did not need any structural changes, but did need a character and a story. New York is so much fun, but it can be tough. I wanted a space that would be a refuge from the busy metropolis. I asked Kishani if she was up for the challenge. A day after the place was legally mine, Kishani and I walked through the empty apartment, and I told her my idea: a Paris-inspired pied-à-terre. When I first started modeling, I lived in Europe: Germany, London, and Paris. I fell in love with the French capital and always wanted to own an apartment there. It wasn't realistic, so if I couldn't have an apartment in Paris, I'd bring Paris to my apartment.

A week later, Kishani and I started our second project together: we flew to the city on the Seine. Why not go straight to the source? The timing was perfect. I had to go to Paris for a day of work, so we decided to stay an additional four and shop the markets for furniture that would fit our theme. Believe it or not, Kishani and I finished the apartment in those four days; it had to be some kind of world record. I know it sounds fun and romantic, but I'm not going to lie: it wasn't. The weather was dismal. It was bitterly cold and depressingly gray, and it rained the entire time. We were soaked head to toe every day. As a matter of fact, one night Kishani and I dressed up to go to a party and none of the hotel staff even recognized us. But don't get me wrong; I still love Paris.

We worked from dawn until dusk, starting the morning off with cappuccinos and croissants and ending the day with hot tea and a warm bath. We concentrated our efforts in two areas: the stalls in Les Puces de Saint-Ouen, and a fantastic trade warehouse just outside the area. Like prospectors, we scoured the flea market stalls (which are an assortment of vintage boutiques, secondhand shops, antiques vendors, independent artists, and informal galleries) for diamonds in the rough. We might not have won any beauty contests while we were there, but our shopping excursions were prosperous and productive. We had several eureka moments, and when you encounter that special piece, it's an adrenaline rush. I know, it's just furniture shopping, but it can be truly satisfying.

Some of the items we bought were inexpensive, and others were investment pieces, but each one tells a story. I remember we were searching and searching for the dining table. It was an important piece; it needed to anchor the room—but we couldn't find one we liked. On the afternoon of our last day in Paris, we walked into a stall and saw what we first thought to be a pretty table with a nice patina; it was the right shape, size, and weight but appeared fairly average. And then we looked down. There were these

substantial legs with oversize, intricately carved griffins at the feet. Wow—now, that was our table. We had a similar experience looking for a sofa. What was at first glance a beat-up, worn-out, dingy sofa was, upon closer inspection, a significant piece—regal in shape, elegant in proportion, and delicate in design. We knew we didn't want it as it was, but we knew we wanted it. We shipped it to the States and had it re-covered to reveal its original majesty. I love this sofa. My mom loves this sofa. My super loves this sofa. And I'm pretty sure my future children will love this sofa. It's that beautiful, but understand: it was a diamond in the rough.

And that is why I love working with Kishani. She has the ability to see the hidden beauty in almost anything. Maybe a piece simply needs to be sanded and stained, re-covered, updated, painted, or polished. Maybe it's a modern piece but would look interesting with an antique finish. Maybe it's a French-country design but would look rock-and-roll if painted a bright color and glazed. What she has (and what she has helped develop in me) is vision. The ability to see potential. And that is what Kishani will teach you. How to make a space truly your own. How to reinvent what you have if you're on a tight budget or how to start from scratch if you're not. Kishani can coax out and cultivate her clients' individual styles and signatures.

We are currently working on our fourth design project together; it's no easier than before and no less work, but I'm enjoying the process. She won't impose her personal taste on your personal space. I'm always disappointed when I see that, when I walk into someone's home and it doesn't look like them. It's too "designed." You won't get that with Kishani. She has helped me to explore and expand my design eye, to take chances, and to trust myself. With her, I've learned how to customize, to mix and match styles and eras, and to use my imagination. She has also made me aware that you can find great pieces in so many places today, whether in traditional retail stores, online, or elsewhere. I still make mistakes; you might have to repaint a wall several times to get it right (or, in the case of my walk-in closet, five times). The two of us can spend days debating fabrics or sconces, but at the end of the day, Kishani has the final say because she is talented.

Whatever your space, your style, or your budget, Kishani gives you the tools and the insider information to do it yourself, to individualize your environment, and to emerge with a place you'll love and love to share.

CHAPTER ONE

inspiration
+
perspiration

Where do design ideas come from? There's no easy answer to that question. It's definitely not a straight line from point A, an empty, lackluster room, to point B, a wonderfully layered space full of things you love. I think there's a little bit of magic—an unexpected spark of inspiration—that happens with every project. It could be a spread in a magazine, an ad at a bus stop, a colorful array of fruit at a farmer's market, or a collection of old wine jugs. That just-right object or glimmer of an idea becomes the catalyst that gives me direction. When I work with clients, I never have a plan before meeting them. My first visit gives me insight into who they are, what they like, and what's important to them. And that flash of inspiration might just come from one of their own mementos, like a postcard from a special trip or a teapot handed down from Grandma. That's what happened with one of my very first clients.

He had no idea what direction he wanted to go style-wise in his new home, so I asked him what one thing he loved most in his last house. He had a soft spot for a classic black-and-white photo of the Rat Pack, which he said made him feel like relaxing and drinking a martini. Bingo! We brought in comfortable chairs that channeled that midcentury lounge vibe and built him a bachelor pad that was unfussy yet old-Hollywood glam, just like the Rat Pack, who are now keeping watch over the room from that very photograph.

But interior design isn't all magic and stardust. There's a lot of legwork involved, and that's where the perspiration comes in. Before you start spending on new furniture and accessories, you need to figure out what you like and how you want your space to look.

Spend time studying. Flip through tons of design magazines and books to find images that speak to you. When you compile a big stack of pictures, some patterns should emerge. Once

you find that common thread, you'll know how to describe the look you love, whether it's beachy modern eclectic, midcentury monochromatic, or French bohemian.

Create a style file. After you've narrowed your focus and have the vocabulary to describe what you like, it's time to start browsing (or "doing research," as I call it). Pull samples of fabrics and colors that fit your style; take a snapshot of a gorgeous vintage sofa or a cool Moroccan side table. Collect all these clippings on an inspiration board until you have a cohesive look.

Dedicate design space. Give yourself room to bring all your inspirations together, spread out your pictures and swatches, and start planning. Seeing all the things you love in one place will help you begin to visualize a space and notice color palettes and themes emerging. It may also bring to light some areas that require more thought, which are important to work out when you're still in the early planning stage.

Believe me, it's worth it to take the time to gather everything together and discover what inspires you. When you're impulsive and impatient, making purchases without a plan in mind, you're more likely to end up with buyer's remorse or go through a million paint colors before finding the right one. With so many options, it can be overwhelming if you don't have focus from the get-go. If you invest the time up front and hone your style now, it will be much easier to make those choices later. Yes, it's work. But it's fun work!

Here are some examples of the diverse (and sometimes wacky) things that have inspired my own designs.

Color

Color fuels me like nothing else. Just flipping through paint fan decks can stimulate more ideas than I can shake a stir stick at. It's always awe-inspiring to see the spectrum of options—pale, saturated, neutral, and bold—laid out before you, and to realize the combinations you can create with them are truly limitless.

Nature

Don't overlook the great outdoors when you're searching for inspiration. Take notice of the rustic bark on a log, or flowers and plants that you like. Even the natural raw materials at a showroom, like gorgeous, iridescent marble, could fire up an idea for a seafoam-hued bathroom or a dining room with a custom marble-topped table.

Textiles

I love fabric shops, and picking out textiles always comes at the beginning of my process. Just browsing through the bolts, looking at colors, textures, and patterns, can help you develop a concept for a room. You should also check out ethnic textiles, like vibrant Indian saris and Mexican blankets, which you can turn into pillows or use as throws. They often have lovely embellished details, such as beaded trims and elaborate embroidery, and are fairly inexpensive.

LICIOUS SYRUP

SINCE
1935

PREPARED BY
T. G. KIAT & CO (PTE) LTD
SINGAPORE.

Ethnic Shops

When you're looking for ideas, stopping by unusual stores or places outside your normal routine can help you think outside the box. I'm like a kid in a candy shop when I stumble on some colorful trinkets. I find inspiration everywhere: jewelry in an import store, the treats at an Indian sweetshop, kitschy silk flowers in Los Angeles's Little Mexico district. Objects like woven friendship bracelets, papier-mâché animal sculptures, and painted guitars all channel a cheerful Latin vibe, and their strong, playful use of color always grabs me. Even the vibrant packages and labels at an ethnic grocery store—or the textures of exotic produce like bitter melon and ginger—could spark a design idea. I've even interpreted a basic staple, such as a sack of rice, into a French-country look, with rustic touches like burlap pillows. You just never know how a flash of inspiration will translate into a real-life design.

· · ·

Inspiration can be found anywhere you look. Open yourself up and notice what appeals to you, whether you're on the street, at the zoo, or at a farmer's market. These seemingly unrelated clues are key to creating a home that speaks to you and makes you happy.

Decorator's Studio

Here in my office, it is important for me to feel at home. I can work pretty crazy hours, so it needed to feel comfortable, clean, and bright—an escape from the chaos of my day. I picked a soothing light-purple hue for the main room, which is where I meet with clients, and made sure to build in plenty of storage to keep it looking organized and professional. In the private back room, where I go to get work done alone, I went for a darker, moodier purple on the walls and brought in personal furnishings. I also made room for a daybed so the space can double as a guest room.

In my office, I surround myself with things I love and keep everything superorganized so I can locate a sample at a moment's notice. And because I meet with clients here, the space has to express my taste and give them an idea of how I work.

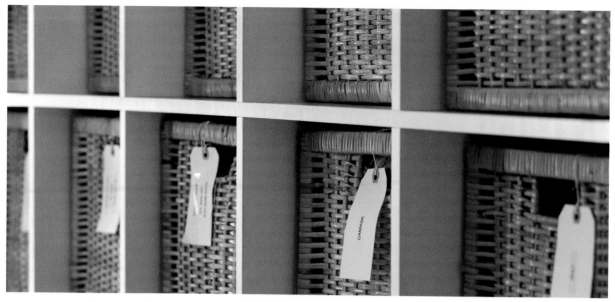

I knew I needed two desks, plus a table at which to meet with clients. But keeping my many textile, wallpaper, and tile samples accessible and organized in a beautiful way was essential, too. My chic and inexpensive solution: a basic storage unit from Ikea filled with matching wicker baskets—each one clearly labeled with a simple shipping tag from an office supply store.

This antique Chinese art deco rug was the inspiration for the entire vibe and palette of the room. I love the unexpected combination of chartreuse, pink, blue, and purplish gray. Plus, it has the coolest provenance—it once belonged to Linda Ronstadt!

These vivid blue decanters pick up on those tones in my rug.

OPPOSITE: My inspiration board contains more than just paint and fabric swatches. I add jewelry, bits and bobs like tassels, and photographs that express a vibe I'm interested in exploring.

LEFT AND BELOW: This dresser with acrylic-fronted drawers allows me to clearly see what's inside, from decorative switch plates to rug samples.

RIGHT: Tile samples get tucked away in attractive metal bins.

BELOW: All work and no play makes for a dull office. I displayed an unusual antique Santos cage doll and a crystal ball filled with pink glitter to keep the feeling fun and light.

LEFT: Etched and hand-painted, this sculptural lamp found on Craigslist really represents my design philosophy. You can find great pieces at any price point and then customize them to your liking. Here I added green, teardrop-shaped wood bobble trim to the shade to create contrast and interest.

BELOW: Initially, I was drawn to peacocks because of their vibrant tail feathers and showy personalities. Later, I realized they have a lot of symbolism in the culture of Sri Lanka, where my family is originally from. I think maybe I knew that deep down somewhere in my subconscious.

OPPOSITE: This is basically the room that eBay built. First I found the art deco brass banker's desk, and then the Chinese rug from the same time period. Put together, they gave off a film noir vibe, so I went for a dark and moody feel with some glam touches, like the Indian peacock mirror. I also found the cushy chair (which I later had reupholstered in velvet) on the auction site. Shopping on eBay is always such a thrill for me because I often score things for a price far below their worth. This rug should have cost ten times what I paid.

LEFT: This geisha lamp, found as part of a pair on eBay for forty dollars, brings another Asian touch to the room. The original colors were pretty crazy, but I repainted the base in hues that complemented my office, and now it fits right in.

BELOW LEFT: An antique cabinet on the opposite side of the room has cool, hand-silvered, convex-mirrored panels. I spotted it at an antique shop and had to have it. Look closely and you can see all the interesting reflections in the slub glass. Personally, I like mirrored finishes to have an aged look and will replace new mirrors with a custom mercury-mix mirror to add some much-needed speckles and dark spots.

BELOW RIGHT: Inexpensive art can be found anywhere if you spend a little time looking. This midcentury Syroco mirrored sunburst went for just ten dollars on eBay. A couple coats of gold spray paint gave it an eye-catching gleam.

OPPOSITE: Visiting friends and family would occasionally spend the night on this plush daybed. I found it at an online retailer and refinished it in black to give it a more colonial look. The quilted coverlet and the grouping of pillows add a touch of texture and pattern.

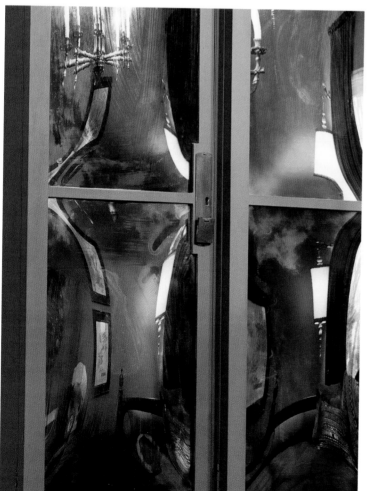

....

prep

+

prime

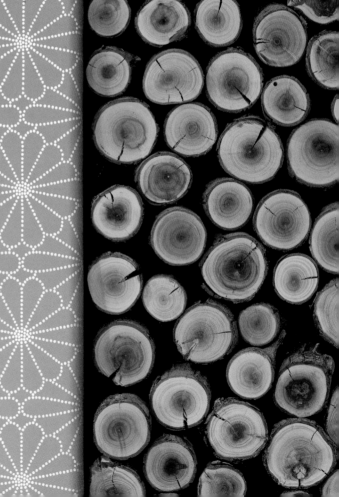

Preparation and planning—though they sound as exciting as watching paint dry—are the real foundation of any successful design. You have to dig deeper, moving past appearance, to think about what you really need from your space and how you will spend time there. My goal is to make sure every square inch of my clients' homes gets used and enjoyed. What's the point of creating a beautiful room if it winds up sitting empty? Or if you end up with a garage full of pieces that just don't work? To prevent that from happening, I map out my clients' needs, take loads of measurements, and figure out detailed room plans. Beyond that, I take this time to start thinking about, and get the ball rolling on, any structural fixes or updates that will affect the architecture of the house. That basic framework needs to be in place before furniture is brought in. Every house has its quirks, but this is where careful planning makes all the difference. For example, if I know I need a storage unit to fit an odd space, I can order a custom piece and factor the timing and cost into the project. In short, these practical steps make the whole process run smoothly and help you make your inspirations become reality.

Designate a purpose for the room. Unless you're lucky enough to have a mansion, there's a good chance most rooms will need to serve multiple functions. Does your dining room need to double as a home office? Do you need a playroom by day, living room by night? It's also important to think outside the blueprint. Just because an architect labeled the space between four walls "dining room" doesn't mean you have to dine there. Be flexible, look at each space with fresh eyes, and you'll find a way to make it meet your needs.

Make architectural changes. Does the structure of the room harmonize with its new purpose or aesthetic? If not, now's the time to do any needed construction, whether that means adding moldings or wainscoting, refinishing the floors, or installing shelving. It's so much easier to take care of this potentially messy work before you have a house full of furniture that needs to be moved around or put into storage. I always pick out flooring at the beginning of every design job. It's a choice that can literally form the foundation of a room's style, whether you pick wide, distressed oak planks that capture a

French-country look, or highly polished, ebony-stained walnut to set a modern tone. Each type of wood has its own character, and the finish you choose can develop it even further.

Create a space plan. For me, designing a room layout is kind of like solving a puzzle. There may be more than one solution, but if you spend enough time with it, one answer will clearly rise to the top. Here's the key: measure all the walls, windows, and doors, then make a to-scale drawing of your room. Now you can sketch out different configurations to see what works best. Is your living room big enough for two conversation areas plus a library nook? You don't need to be a great artist or a professional renderer to do this; even a basic sketch on a napkin can help you realize the limitations of the space. If drawing just isn't your thing, try an online room-planning tool. There are many, but Google's SketchUp is one of the easiest to use. As you decide on furniture placement and ideal sizes, note specific measurements (e.g., "sofa for den must be between seventy-two and eighty-four inches long"). And remember to take into account your storage needs, both large and small. This way, when you go out armed with your shopping list and notebook full of measurements, you'll stay on track and won't be lured into buying anything you don't need or that doesn't fit your space.

LEFT AND OPPOSITE: This living room reminds me of "Goldilocks and the Three Bears": Full-size couches were too massive, but love seats were too small. Custom, smaller-scale gray-linen sofas were the just-right fix. Pink accents pop against the gray and, along with the glitzy chandelier, showcase my client's girly, feminine side.

Order custom pieces. Once you've laid out your room plan, you should know if you'll need custom pieces made. Maybe one-size-fits-all furniture *doesn't* fit your room, or there's a specific style you can't find at a retail store or flea market. That's when you need the services of a craftsman you trust. Like all good things, quality workmanship takes time, so plan ahead if you can, do research at showrooms, and discuss timing and budget with your contractor. The goal is to get your order in as early as possible so that one piece won't hold up the rest of your project's timeline. Keep in mind that handmade pieces—like a hand-poured concrete table—can take two months or more to build from scratch. The same applies to any custom wood moldings or furniture with labor-intensive hand-carved details. But it's well worth the wait for something made exactly the way you want.

• • •

Planning out your home's design can be a lengthy process. But taking this essential time to figure out your needs and how to make the most of your home will pay off in the long run. Believe me, it will end up saving your sanity—and your budget.

ABOVE: Over the year that I worked on the project, the room truly evolved. It started out very designed—almost showroom-like. But as the homeowner and I shopped together for accessories, she became more comfortable trusting her instincts, which made the space that much cozier and more personal. It's often those little things, like a hobnail goblet (something her mother collects), old books, or even an odd collection of sculpted hands, that give a room the most meaning and make it a place where you want to spend time.

OPPOSITE: Sumptuous, custom blue-velvet chairs take center stage in this eclectic dining area. We searched for a simple table that wouldn't draw attention away from them and that could fit the small space. Since the first floor of the home has such an open plan, it was important to make sure everything flowed from one room to the next, like the console that bridges the space between the dining and seating areas.

Hollywood Hills Mediterranean

This client and I first met when she was working with another designer, who excelled at the shopping part of decorating. Space planning wasn't exactly his forte, so that's how I ended up partnering with him on the project. The house was especially challenging: many of the rooms were broken up oddly and standard furniture just didn't fit. The first designer had been looking for ages for a sofa that would work in her living room. He hunted around flea markets, stores, and showrooms without any luck, and finally said to me with exasperation, "This is going to take all year!" That's when I reminded him that we could just have exactly what we wanted custom-made in the exact right size. Problem solved! I went on to work with the client to finish her home, approaching it like a puzzle.

A long, massive sitting room with structural columns that couldn't be removed posed another space-planning challenge. To make those columns more of a feature than a drawback, I had them wrapped in distressed wood veneer. Creating a main seating area around the fireplace, as well as a reading nook with a wingback chair in the corner, helped break up the space.

The look of this room evolved over time with a few seemingly small decorative changes. We hung subtle metallic wallpaper (seen on the previous page), swapped the accent pillows for ones in shades of blue (previous page), and brought in new artwork. Once it was filled in with stacked logs, the odd recess beside the fireplace added visual interest.

Bold Cole & Son wallpaper in a botanical print became the
foundation for the office's bohemian yet feminine look. Plush
textures, like the deep shag rug and luxurious button-tufted-
velvet sofa, along with lots of colorful accessories, help capture
an informal, creative vibe. With plenty of comfortable seating, the
space is perfect for solo brainstorming or a group meeting for the
homeowner's jewelry design business.

LEFT: These massive white closet doors were a huge blank canvas. Adding molding in a Moorish star design and cool square pulls gave them an architectural presence. And since the room lacked wall space to hang paintings or photos, the doors almost function as art.

BELOW: Dressing the glam white Ultrasuede bed in a lived-in, vintage linen duvet cover and shams with lightly shredded hems creates a soft and serene effect. A touch of pattern—ikat accent pillows in shades reminiscent of a peacock's tail—brings vibrancy that keeps the mostly monochromatic room from feeling too sleepy.

OPPOSITE: A grouping of beautiful old jewelry boxes anchors a pretty scene on a dresser. Since my client runs her own jewelry line, the boxes are functional, too. But plenty of baubles go on display in dishes or on a tray. They're just too lovely to always keep tucked away.

Vintage remix

ABOVE AND LEFT: Paint transformed this once stuck-in-the-seventies kitchen. We saved the previously orange-stained wood cabinets by refinishing them in white and adding new hardware to give a much more modern look. Carrera marble on the counters and backsplash was a nice upgrade from the old tile. To balance all the white in the room, we went for a dark-gray hue on the walls and the ceiling and for ebony-finished floors, which added dramatic contrast and depth. It's a very chic kitchen, but the Japanese lucky-cat sculpture on the windowsill gives it a bit of levity.

OPPOSITE: The ceiling was an odd height that didn't work with standard fixtures. Rather than settle for too-short or too-long lights, we had custom glass-globe pendants made.

An ikat-print throw pillow picks up on the color of the gorgeous coral bougainvillea growing nearby.

OPPOSITE: A bench or a couch would have taken up too much precious space on this narrow balcony. The solution: a long, built-in stucco bench that works with the architecture and looks like it's an original part of the house. By packing lots of seating into a small footprint, we opened up the rest of the space for more comfortable entertaining. Two outdoor wicker chairs form an intimate seating area at the opposite end of the balcony.

The Chinese figurine, a gift from my client's mom, has a meditative pose that seems appropriate for the serene outdoor space.

Ornate metal furniture would have felt clichéd on the patio of my client's classic Mediterranean home. New England–style weathered-wood loungers offer a break from the obvious, and playful polka dots and colorful serving pieces bring a lively 1950s vibe.

Bamboo light fixtures, painted a coral hue and modified to work outdoors, remind me of carousels. The seeded-glass panels reflect the light in a dreamy way, creating an enchanting effect at night.

I love this whimsical mermaid vase. Though it looks antique, I found it at an online retailer called At West End. Every table should have something unique and unexpected on it.

OPPOSITE: The homeowner wanted an outdoor dining space for casual meals with friends. To get this charming vintage look, we paired a rustic farmhouse table with humble metal folding chairs and set out vivid antique blue glassware.

CHAPTER THREE

skimp

+

splurge

Pompeii and the Roman Villa
ART AND CULTURE AROUND THE BAY OF NAPLES

Here's the good news: you don't need a sky-high budget to pull off great design. While some designers specialize in luxury homes, buying only the best (read: most expensive) of everything, that's just not me. I see the potential in things no matter what they cost and find real satisfaction every time I score an inexpensive item in an off-the-beaten-path place. My philosophy in a nutshell: money won't buy you style. And when it comes down to it, even my most well-to-do clients have a certain budget in mind. I'll frequent Craigslist, eBay, flea markets, and chain retailers as often as I do designer showrooms. I find such satisfaction in reinventing pieces and making minor tweaks that transform the standard into the truly special. All of my projects combine a mix of high and low and blend genres so that there's always an element of surprise in a room.

To keep spending in line, the secret is deciding where you need to shell out and where you can scale back. While there are no hard-and-fast rules saying, "Spend here" and "Save your cash here," these strategies work for me.

Spend on what you'll use most. Just as you might not mind splurging on a classic jacket or a hot pair of jeans that gets regular rotation in your wardrobe, it's worth it to spend on what you will use constantly in your home. To me, a truly comfortable sofa and supersoft bedding are worth a little extra.

Know that custom will cost you. Shades made to fit an odd-size window, or a chair done in special-order fabric, necessitate a bump in the price. When you're on a tight budget, go custom only when it's absolutely necessary.

Should you love it or leave it? If you tend to be an overly spontaneous shopper, institute a twenty-four-hour waiting period. Then, if you're still thinking about it after your shopping time-out, go ahead and buy it.

Work with what you have. It may be in our instincts to start fresh, but repurposing the quality items you already own is green and wallet-friendly. Repaint, reupholster, or even just relocate a piece to a different room and it can end up feeling brand-new.

• • •

No matter how much you have to spend, creative thinking—and a little bit of legwork—will ultimately help you balance your purchases and stay within your budget. Shopping with an open mind, whether it's on eBay or Craigslist, at a thrift store or a retail chain, or in a designer showroom, allows you to see the potential in a piece that could be perfect with just a tweak here or there. They say necessity is the mother of invention. It's true! Smart spending has spawned some of my most original ideas, and those are what make a space truly personal and dynamic.

LEFT: Using secondhand furniture allowed us to furnish this dining room on a modest budget.

OPPOSITE: We kept many of the homeowners' living room furnishings—traditional, well-made pieces—but spent on new silk drapes and elegant accessories to make the look cohesive.

Eco-Chic Co-op

How far will I go for a deal? This project put me to the test. The homeowner and I were pulling together the decor of her new house for a TV show about green makeovers, so we had a very limited budget—and not much time to make it happen. Eco-friendly design calls for lots of thrifting; you can find great furniture and accessories that might otherwise end up in a landfill. So we pored over Craigslist and eBay day and night and visited every flea market in town. Because of the tight schedule, there was no time to reupholster or refinish anything, which meant tracking down furniture with good bones *and* decent upholstery. We scoured Los Angeles thrift shops and even trekked out to Echo Park and other far-flung neighborhoods. Sometimes our Craigslist buys were sixty to seventy miles out of town! (Still, that's a far cry from the distances most newly manufactured furniture travels to get to your local showroom.) That's what I call putting in the legwork. It was challenging to find pieces that fit the overall aesthetic we wanted, but keeping an open mind helped. For example, though I was on the lookout for a buffet, I found a 1950s cupboard that I loved, and it worked just as well in the space, so it didn't feel like a trade-off. Working almost entirely with vintage, we naturally mixed up eras and styles for a funky, collected look. The result was cohesive and interesting.

An industrial credenza serves as a buffet *and* a discreet home office. The homeowner's printer and other supplies are tucked out of sight in the drawers.

LEFT: Near the entrance, an art deco desk partners with a country-style chair with a needlepoint seat. Diverse accessories, ranging from a 1960s lamp to an Asian vase to a 1930s painting, make the vignette especially interesting.

BELOW LEFT: A beautiful, low midcentury modern dresser, dramatically styled with a large-scale lamp, became the focal point of the bedroom.

BELOW RIGHT: Materials and construction blew the budget on this modest bathroom renovation, so we had to get creative when it came to the details. Instead of buying a plain, boring shower curtain, I found this cool plastic beaded room divider and hung it from the hooks, layering it over a basic white liner. It gives the room a glamorous, art deco feel and cost next to nothing.

OPPOSITE: The linoleum checkerboard floor and antique stove called for a 1950s diner look. A vintage dinette set and simple faux roman shades in gauzy black linen finish off the retro kitchen. Window treatments can be very costly, especially with so many windows to cover, but these were done on a shoestring. The fabric is stapled to a thin strip of wood cut to fit the window frame, and my seamstress created pintuck gathers to give the shades additional detail and texture.

Patience really paid off in this house. It takes time to find the right furniture in the right style and scale. In fact, it took two months just to locate the perfect Persian rug in shades of bright blue, brown, and tan. The olive button-tufted wingbacks and fifties-style sofa (both Craigslist finds) help set the midcentury eclectic vibe. And while we tried to limit retail purchases because money was tight, these simple light-filtering drapes from Cost Plus World Market were an inexpensive exception.

Bel Air Mediterranean

Once in a while, I pick up where another designer has left off. Rather than scrap the previous investments, my task is to incorporate them and complete the look. Since the client had already spent a great deal on furnishings for her ten-thousand-square-foot home, this was especially important. Choice accessories went a long way in the transformation.

In such a large-scale room, having several separate seating areas was key, but the collection of couches, benches, and chairs felt random and disconnected. I brought in neutral silk draperies and a huge custom rug that complemented the colors of the furniture and tied everything together.

LEFT: The grand architectural details of the home called for drama and elegance, which we created with an extravagant rock-crystal chandelier.

OPPOSITE AND BELOW RIGHT: In another corner of the room, a massive World War II–era aluminum palm tree, saved from a now-defunct Hollywood restaurant, emphasizes the lofty, twenty-foot-high ceiling. It's a little bit quirky, and it offsets the more traditional furnishings to give the room a younger, livelier feel.

BELOW LEFT: With its timeworn finish, this ancient angel lamp adds a dose of old-world character.

LEFT: In a refined home like this, even the accessories should be well curated. Here, each item has delicate details that play up the elegance of the room: an etched gold vase, a lotus flower hand-carved out of stone, a mother-of-pearl-inlaid curio box, and a potted orchid on a carved wood tray.

BELOW LEFT: A mix of accessories from diverse cultures—an Indian box, a Thai hand sculpture, and a mercury glass vase—creates an interesting scene.

BELOW RIGHT AND OPPOSITE: On a silk-upholstered ottoman, braided trim with an embellished fringe resonates with the room's grandeur. In general, the more ornate the architecture of a house, the more elaborate you can go with the ornamentation.

PREVIOUS SPREAD: Extravagant artwork would have been overkill here. Instead, an oversize mirror enhances the light and color in the room.

LEFT: This amazing Chinese art deco rug became the foundation for the dining room. It wasn't at all what the client expected, but she fell in love at first sight with the unusual mix of orange, raspberry, and sapphire. Pulling the blue from the rug, we re-covered the chairs in a matching sumptuous silk velvet.

BELOW LEFT: A room this glamorous called for an equally spectacular light fixture. We brought in another custom chandelier, this one adorned with unique, smoky gray European rock crystals, to create a glitzy, modern edge. Complementary sconces add even more sparkle to the room.

BELOW RIGHT: I found this black lacquered credenza with goatskin-covered drawers to serve as a buffet and a bar. It's a true one-of-a-kind piece, and the glam materials perfectly suit the rest of the room's design.

RIGHT: The architect of this house went superdramatic, combining multiple carved pieces of molding in different styles (dentil, egg-and-dart) to build character. Even if you don't have twenty-foot-high ceilings, moldings can draw the eye up, transforming the look of a room.

BELOW LEFT: I find that animals (even fake ones) bring life into a room. This horse's head, which stands sentry beside the fireplace, reminds me of a chess piece.

BELOW RIGHT: To punch up the excitement in this once-neutral room, we brought in lots of black and white, with a Moroccan inlaid dresser, transitional armchairs in cool glazed leather, and a quirky tree-base side table. Adding contemporary patterns with the zebra ottoman and throw pillows instantly modernized the look.

ABOVE: To add some youth and vibrancy to the sea of neutrals in this family room, I used colorful fabrics. To chase away the conservative vibe and give the room some edge, I fabricated an ebonized coffee table with an antique mirror top and found a glamorous, black lacquered floor lamp. Chinese garden stools and a rattan side table my client already owned enhance the eclectic mix.

RIGHT: Custom pillows made from luxurious fabrics add rich texture and pattern to the sofas.

OPPOSITE: The bedroom has high ceilings and relatively small-scale furniture, so we went with a large, open, and airy chandelier to take up some of the empty space and give the room greater presence.

WALDEN POND, MASSACHUSETTS

This well-made sofa, once solid chenille, felt a little plain for such a richly detailed, sophisticated study. Reupholstered in an eggplant-and-gold-patterned cut velvet, it's now a focal point of the room and contrasts nicely with the smooth leather club chairs. With a few custom-made coordinating pillows, the room feels polished.

This quirky needlepoint dog pillow adds a small dose of camp to the elegant room, demonstrating the homeowner's sense of humor.

When accessorizing in a man's space, look for objects that are useful and not just decorative. Here, a decanter of brandy, a wooden duck decoy, and a match holder—all traditionally masculine items—impart a very East Coast, Ivy League vibe to the room.

LEFT: We placed these elegant ivory-inlaid boxes on the table to accent this opulent entryway without distracting from its grandeur. Functional and decorative, these types of boxes can easily add interest to any space, and different designs can be found at ethnic shops, thrift stores, and chain retailers.

BELOW LEFT: The foyer has impressive fifty-foot-high ceilings, so finding the right-size chandeliers was a challenge. On a trip to London, my client came across this fixture, a modern interpretation of a basket chandelier with cut metal instead of traditional glass or crystal. It was at the perfect scale, and I told her it was well worth the splurge. In fact, I said if she didn't buy it, I would! This might be my favorite light fixture of all time.

BELOW RIGHT AND OPPOSITE: In the breakfast room, small changes made a big difference. We kept the previously chosen draperies and furniture and simply re-covered the chair seats with stitched paisley fabric. Custom lumbar pillows add a graphic touch.

CHAPTER FOUR

....

hunt

+

gather

Now for the fun part: shopping. After discovering the look you want, making a game plan, and mapping out exactly what you need to buy, it's time to start spending. I truly enjoy the search and will hunt high and low—literally—all the way from fancy designer showrooms down to Craigslist, stopping at all the chain stores and online shops in between. Good design is everywhere and at every price point, and I find that mixing up new and vintage, and retail and custom, makes for the most layered, interesting interiors. Remember that you can (and should) personalize furnishings and accessories in order to set your home apart from everyone else's, even if you shop at the same stores. Those custom touches and the unique way you combine things express your personal taste. With that said, there are a few things to keep in mind before you set out to decorate your home.

Don't be a shopping snob. Some of my coolest, most distinctive finds have come from charity shops or Craigslist.

Think outside the box. Look at things with a creative eye and you'll see potential everywhere. Maybe you can turn a vintage printed dress into pillow covers or upholster a bench with burlap flour sacks.

Find tradespeople you trust. If you can imagine it, they can do it. Keep a seamstress on speed dial if your sewing skills aren't up to par, and get to know furniture restorers. That way,

you can buy that tired chair and rest assured it can be lacquered hot pink or reupholstered in a funky fabric.

• • •

As you hunt and gather for your home, keep an open mind and, most of all, have fun! Remember that you're never stuck forever with anything you have. So go ahead and buy that fabulous upholstered chair in a modern print or your favorite color of the moment. After all, if your taste changes in a few years, you can always take it to be reupholstered. Your home should evolve with you.

ABOVE LEFT: This dining table, with its cool, carved griffin feet, was a Paris flea-market find. We stripped the chairs' legs to match the table's natural finish and reupholstered the set in a graphic European velvet.

ABOVE RIGHT: Flea markets are also a great resource for quirky art like this portrait. Displaying the painting on an easel gives the piece prominence in the room, and makes it easy to change out the artwork on a whim.

OPPOSITE: The artwork, *Heaven* by Matthew Heller, fits right into the monochromatic scheme but also adds a young and lighthearted touch that balances the more serious furniture.

OH THINKIN ABOUT ALL OUR YOUNGER YEARS THERE WAS ONLY YOU AND ME WE WERE YOUNG AND WILD AND FREE NOW NOTHIN CAN TAKE YOU AWAY FROM ME WE BEEN DOWN THAT ROAD BEFORE BUT THATS OVER NOW YOU KEEP ME COMIN BACK FOR MORE BABY YOURE ALL THAT I WANT WHEN YOURE LYIN HERE IN MY ARMS IM FINDIN IT HARD TO BELIEVE WERE IN HEAVEN AND LOVE IS ALL THAT I NEED AND I FOUND IT THERE IN YOUR HEART ISNT TOO HARD TO SEE WERE IN HEAVEN OH ONCE IN YOUR LIFE YOU FIND SOMEONE WHO WILL TURN YOUR WORLD AROUND BRING YOU UP WHEN YOURE FEELIN DOWN YEAH NOTHIN COULD CHANGE WHAT YOU MEAN TO ME OH THERES LOTS THAT I COULD SAY BUT JUST HOLD ME NOW CAUSE OUR LOVE WILL LIGHT THE WAY AND BABY YOURE ALL THAT I WANT WHEN YOURE LYIN HERE IN MY ARMS IM FINDIN IT HARD TO BELIEVE WERE IN HEAVEN YEAH LOVE IS ALL I NEED AND I FOUND IT THERE IN YOUR HEART IT ISNT TOO HARD TO SEE WERE IN HEAVEN YEAH IVE BEEN WAITIN FOR SO LONG FOR SOMETHIN TO ARRIVE FOR LOVE TO COME ALONG NOW OUR DREAMS ARE COMIN TRUE THROUGH THE GOOD TIMES AND THE BAD YEAH ILL BE STANDIN THERE BY YOU OH AND BABY YOURE ALL THAT I WANT WHEN YOURE LYIN HERE IN MY ARMS IM FINDIN IT HARD TO BELIEVE WERE IN HEAVEN AND LOVE IS ALL THAT I NEED AND I FOUND IT THERE IN YOUR HEART ISNT TOO HARD TO SEE WERE IN HEAVEN HEAVEN WOAH YOURE ALL THAT I WANT YOURE ALL THAT I NEED

Parisian-Chic Loft

Normally, shopping for the right furniture takes up a good portion of any design job. In this case, we had just four days! My client bought a loft in New York City and decided she wanted to decorate her new place to look like a romantic Parisian flat. In the course of our conversation, she convinced me to head to France with her on a shopping trip. Time was short from the get-go because we had less than three months to get the place ready for a magazine cover shoot. On a two-hour layover in New York on our way to Paris, I ran around the apartment taking measurements, making sketches, and getting a feel for the space. It has one big open living area, so I planned a basic layout, carving a seating area, dining room, and foyer out of the main room. After we arrived in Paris, the race was on. We had four days to shop for the entire apartment, so we put in long hours, waking up when it was still dark to get a head start at the flea markets, skipping meals, and losing sleep. Despite the cold, rainy weather, we were committed to the hunt and wandered from stall to stall with measuring tapes and cameras in our pockets. In addition to the time pressure, I was stressed about making a mistake. After all, at flea markets, there is no return policy. If you buy something in the wrong size, you're out of luck—and a good deal of money after shipping it all the way back to the States. We must have had the shopping gods on our side, though, because everything we bought fit the space perfectly. Being prepared with those haphazard sketches and notes—even if no one else could decipher them—paid off.

Layer upon layer of pattern gives the master bedroom its chic Parisian vibe. The flea market bed, redone in charcoal damask, now has a more youthful, modern feel. Keeping the damask, vintage polka-dot throw and chevron pillows in the same subtle blue-gray palette ensures the disparate patterns complement each other rather than compete. Tone-on-tone floral wallpaper, an opulent chandelier, and luxurious sateen draperies complete the look of decadence.

OPPOSITE: Whimsical pink-polka-dot silk instantly warms the look and feel of vintage metal stools from Paris. Lined up along the breakfast bar, they introduce more color to the gray kitchen. The painted-wood, beaded chandelier and framed botanical prints, all found at a flea market, add even more visual interest.

LEFT: One of my favorite things about flea market shopping is that you can often find high-quality pieces at a price far less than retail. We purchased the chesterfield sofa and wingback chairs and had them reupholstered in rich gray velvets.

BELOW LEFT: This anatomical diagram of a bee, hanging in the foyer, looks to have been plucked straight from a naturalist's study and is quite striking given its size. One large-scale piece of art typically has more impact than a collection of little pictures, especially in a home with high ceilings.

BELOW RIGHT: Classic white subway tile and Carrera marble never go out of style. The sconces, another timeless choice, were found at a chain retailer but outfitted with custom shades. Hand-printed wallpaper ties the bath into the subtle prints in the adjoining bedroom.

LEFT: Printed grasscloth wallpaper brings depth and dimension to this sophisticated powder room. The dark blue-gray hue of the paper also picks up on the subtle ribbons in the Carrera marble countertop. The blue-and-white bowl, bought at auction by the client's mother, lends a more personal touch.

BELOW LEFT: This 1940s lamp had belonged to my client's mother, so it had real personal meaning. Topping it with a soft, custom pleated shade modernized it and complemented its feminine form. Those curves help offset the heavier furniture and masculine blues in the room.

BELOW RIGHT: Arranging items on a tray makes your vignette look purposeful instead of like clutter. This ornate mirrored tray, a thrift shop find, can also be easily whisked out of the way if the ottoman is needed for extra seating.

OPPOSITE: A huge floor mirror on one wall helps to open up and define the dining space.

Cultured Craftsman

This cosmopolitan couple, who are East Coast transplants, wanted to incorporate the furnishings from their old downtown New York City loft into their new house in the Santa Monica area. Tying the old in with the new was essential to helping them, along with their kids and dogs, feel at home. We merged the two coasts by adding lots of vintage pieces, as well as influences from other regions, especially Asia. And because the Craftsman architecture's dark wood can feel heavy, we balanced it with colorful, young, and fun accents. The result? A melting-pot style that is just right for this worldly family.

This turn-of-the-century Craftsman house already had amazing bones and beautiful period tile on the walls. A vintage Asian cabinet complements the architectural style. Adding a few patterned pillows to the plain sofa and bringing in some vases with interesting wood-bark texture gave the room the little bit of complexity it needed without competing with the stunning architecture.

Vintage remix

LEFT: Built-ins are another unique feature of Craftsman homes. This bench beneath the stairs felt a little dark, so we searched at fabric stores for the perfect print and made custom cushions to give the space a brighter, more youthful appeal.

BELOW LEFT: In this once simple bath, vintage fixtures add character. I chose foo dog towel rings, an art deco sconce from a vintage shop, and Victorian-style fixtures in the same warm brass finish.

BELOW RIGHT: A vintage, bohemian hand-painted vase brings a vibrant pop of color to the room.

OPPOSITE: When you can't find what you need, make it. I had a seamstress turn affordable ikat-print fabric into a shower curtain simply by adding grommets along the top.

Tone-on-tone wallpaper with a pattern composed of tiny glass beads brings a subtle sparkle to the bathroom. Vintage accessories such as mercury glass urns and a jewelry box add to the feminine feel.

To save precious nightstand space, my client bought these mercury glass pendants at a retail shop. Replacing the chain with vintage square links gives it an antique vibe.

Quirky accents, like this Asian doll-head vase from eBay, line the bathroom windowsill.

OPPOSITE: In this bedroom full of sandy neutrals, a pretty aqua-blue Murano glass lamp found on eBay brings in a touch of the nearby ocean. We added a custom shade with a graphic diamond pattern that ties the room's sand-and-water palette together.

CHAPTER FIVE

mix

+

match

Confidence is the secret to creating a truly unique space. You need it to successfully combine the styles, cultures, and eras that reflect the taste of the person who lives there. I never want a room to be one-note or easily discernible as having one particular design, just as I wouldn't want to be friends with a completely single-minded person. *Eclectic* may be an overused word, but it most closely describes my point of view. My work is similar to a mash-up of songs: while the individual pieces are familiar, the way they're put together creates a whole new experience. You might get tired of a room that was all indie all the time, but throw in a little pop, jazz, and world, and suddenly it feels exciting, fresh, and new. The truth is people are multifaceted, with interests that lie all over the map. My goal is to create interiors that reveal bits of those interests, blending, say, *Mad Men*–era furniture with Indian textiles and Latin American modern art. There's nothing dynamic about a room that looks like a furniture store vignette, or staying locked into one particular style just because your home happens to be a midcentury ranch. The mix-and-match philosophy is all about uncovering what speaks to you and embracing that diversity. When you trust your instincts and allow yourself the freedom to bring together items you love, things tend to fall into place. And that's how you end up with a vibrant and layered home.

Shop around. Even if you adore everything in a certain store, don't buy all your furnishings in one place. Using a variety of sources will help you get a more authentic feel.

Say no to matching sets. It's a lot more interesting to find a pair of matching chairs that coordinate with a different sofa. Of course, if you're brave enough, you can go totally mismatched, too.

Look for common threads. To blend styles successfully, you should always have one element that ties them together. Look for items that are of a similar scale, vibe, finish, or color to help unify them.

• • •

A mix-and-match philosophy takes a lot of the pressure off of "getting it right" in decorating. There's no need to conform to a certain style or fret over every purchase. Shopping, whether at an antique hardware store or little ethnic shops, can be a source of endless inspiration. Take notice of the things that catch your eye, whether it's the shape and patina of an interesting object or the color and texture of Mexican blankets or Indian saris. If you love it, buy it! Don't spend too much time trying to categorize your style. The most interesting homes incorporate myriad styles in a fun and personal way.

In the kitchen, we took our design cues from the house's Tuscan style, and accessorized with colorful Mediterranean fruits and vegetables. But in the rest of the home, we branched out and tried different aesthetics.

Though there are no Asian influences in the house, a stone Buddha head sculpture inspired me to create a Zen feel for the outdoor space.

OPPOSITE: In this couple's home, classic pieces take on a more bohemian vibe with the addition of modern accessories and artwork, all in a chic black-and-white palette.

Tuscan Modern Townhouse

When we began working together, this homeowner planned to flip her 1970s Tuscan townhouse in the Los Angeles hills. Typically, a flipper's goal is to make a home deliberately impersonal in order to appeal to the broadest range of potential buyers. She wanted to give the house a cool and inviting vibe but didn't want to spend too much on the staging. So we bought most of the furniture from affordable retailers like Crate & Barrel, Pottery Barn, and Z Gallerie. As we went along, I convinced her to buy some vintage rugs that were also reasonably priced but so much more unique—they looked like expensive antiques. She suddenly saw her home in a new light and decided to stay put. Then we focused on finding accessories that expressed her style and totally erased the bland, catalog feel. While she may have chosen the wrong designer to help her create a "safe" interior, I like to think it all worked out in the end.

Here's proof that pieces with chain store provenance don't have to look cookie-cutter. The dining set and artwork from Z Gallerie and a light fixture from Pottery Barn feel suddenly special and unique when paired with a one-of-a-kind rug found on eBay.

This odd foyer, positioned between the kitchen and the family room, posed a challenge. Since it's the entry, it needs to set the tone for the entire house, but the client also wanted a breakfast room. To serve both purposes, I staged it as a dramatic seating area that's a little bit formal but still comfortable to sit in and enjoy a morning cup of coffee.

In the bedroom, the sophisticated green-gray hue on the walls and layers of textured white bedding create a serene and restful vibe.

LEFT: The powder room lacked character, so we brought in a sink cabinet with ornately carved details. The elaborate curlicues on the hammered-metal mirror and the carved candle sconces both echo that fluidity.

BELOW LEFT: I love the pattern and pops of turquoise in this rug, an eBay find.

BELOW RIGHT: Because it was designed when my client was still planning to flip the house, we kept the elements in the master bath simple and chic. A pedestal for her toiletries and a vase of flowers go a long way to personalize the space.

Passed down from her grandmother, this old-fashioned cut-crystal lighter and ashtray bring a little shimmer to my client's family room.

Antique books have so much character in and of themselves, but they also make great pedestals for displaying sculptural objects.

OPPOSITE AND ABOVE: Even in rooms that contain matching sets of furniture, you can mix things up with vintage accessories and custom details to create interest. This sitting room has a beautiful, one-of-a-kind antique rug and handmade pillows that help counter the plainness of so much beige upholstery.

We upgraded the patio furniture set with custom cushions and pillows made with rugged Sunbrella. The vivid turquoise accent color came from an unlikely source: the garden hose. It felt appropriate to pull from something so intrinsic to the outdoor space, so we used doses of its pretty blue-green hue throughout the area, on everything from pillows to planters.

London Calling

In this open, airy, quintessential Los Angeles home, my clients

had planned to keep everything white to embrace their light,

bright environment. To make this English couple feel at home,

I pictured a blend of old-world British style and the modern

London look. In the end, we went for a black-and-white palette

punctuated with pops of color—namely, red orange—to keep

the look cohesive. In order to prevent the scheme from feeling

repetitive, we brought in lots of different textures, fabrics, and

unique light fixtures, all of which helped cultivate a stylish,

bohemian vibe that felt appropriate for this artsy family.

Industrial stools and a retro 1940s
pendant add so much character to the
all-white kitchen. You can match your
fixtures to the era of your home, but I
like the juxtaposition of an antique light
in a modern house.

LEFT: In this entry, styles collide. I was pleased that my clients had the confidence to combine a traditional chandelier with a contemporary zebra-hide rug, a shabby-chic mirror, and an antique console. Even this chair blurs design lines: it's a very trad shape but with avant-garde, abstract leather upholstery. (The pattern on the chair, which once belonged to the fashion designer Paul Smith, is a riff on the British flag.)

BELOW LEFT: Look closely and you'll notice the level of detail in this chandelier. Instead of plain iron, the arms have decorative scrollwork and welded-on leaves. Even the glass bobeches are etched with floral and Greek key motifs.

BELOW RIGHT: We arranged these two traditional chairs casually in the corner of the living room and deliberately chose to put the lamp and vase on the floor in order to imbue the conversation area with a slightly bohemian, unstructured vibe.

RIGHT: Massive gold-toned rams' heads make an unusual base for a dining table, but because the other elements of the room remain so understated, it works.

BELOW: In this black-and-white family room, we used a variety of furniture styles, like an overstuffed sofa and a bergère chair, to keep it from feeling one-note. Leaving the guitars out for my clients (she's a professional musician; he plays for fun) adds an artistic quality to the room.

Mirrors framed with reclaimed pressed tin salvaged from old ceilings, classic penny-tile floors, and unique tin Jieldé sconces add a vintage warmth to the second bath. I like how the aged finishes contrast with the futuristic woven-vinyl wallpaper with an opalescent sheen.

Scoring a piece like this seventies glam dressing table on eBay makes my day—and the room. I re-covered the stool with faux ostrich skin, and now it looks so cool and chic, you can imagine a movie starlet putting on her makeup here.

Here in the bedroom, the absence of color *becomes* a color. Since the furnishings all recede, the right light fixtures—heavy gold Murano leaf sconces and a seventies brass and lucite banker's floor lamp—really come to the forefront.

OPPOSITE: An ebony, marble-topped chest fills the space in this small vestibule between the living room and master bedroom. On top, a black-and-white vignette brings character without color. Most people would display an acting award on a mantel, but not this client. Demonstrating that he has kept a sense of humor about himself, he turned the sleek figural sculpture into an elegant hat rack.

Miracle Mile Revival

Oftentimes, renters don't bother decorating their homes, which is a huge missed opportunity. Luckily, this client wasn't one of those design commitment-phobes. She wanted to make over her 1930s flat, but there were limitations. We couldn't change the bathroom tile, or even the dining room light fixture, and were on a tight budget. To cut down on costs, she did a great deal of legwork herself, which made the project a fun and collaborative process. The apartment had very traditional and elaborate architectural details that just weren't meshing with my client's contemporary pieces, so we reinvented them with new upholstery and fabric. Going Hollywood glam and decidedly feminine helped to reconcile that style divide.

Rich red on the walls gives the foyer a regal feel. To continue that mood, we paired a rococo-style mirror with a cabriole-leg cabinet. Modern white accessories, such as a Jonathan Adler giraffe lamp and a simple planter, help to offset the more ornate, antique style of the furniture.

PREVIOUS SPREAD AND LEFT: The sofas, once ultramod in white Ultrasuede fabric, were redone in luxe, charcoal gray velvet. With hot-pink accent pillows, a Lucite table, and a faux-zebra-hide rug, the room now feels simultaneously old and new.

BELOW LEFT: In the bedroom, we softened the hard lines of the angular metal bed with a wispy white canopy and an ornate crystal chandelier. My client was torn between two different purple hues for the walls, so we used both, installing a chair rail and painting the deeper shade below it and the lighter one above it. This dramatic ombré effect actually draws the eye up, making the ceiling feel higher. While the room is still unabashedly girly, simple white accents and accessories temper the result.

BELOW RIGHT: Here, a *handira* (a textured Moroccan wedding blanket) was repurposed as a floor covering. Its texture, along with the feminine mauve hue on the walls, works to balance out the hard lines of the contemporary wood table and Eames molded-plastic chairs.

OPPOSITE: Instead of a plain shower curtain, a beaded room divider adds an art deco feel and complements the black bands of tile. It's a trick I've used before that works especially well in a bath with vintage tile like this one.

textile

+

pattern

Fabric shops are some of the first places I turn to for inspiration, because the textiles you choose will have a big impact on your space. Furniture upholstery, window treatments, floor coverings, and all those other soft goods make a room feel layered and interesting. Often as I'm browsing through fabrics or looking at rugs online, I find a pattern so spectacular that it ends up serving as the catalyst for an entire room's design. Other times it's a swatch that I'll end up using as an accent on a pillow or a lampshade to add a special detail. On a functional level, textiles provide warmth. Imagine your home without them. Hard (literally), right? You'd have nothing but wood furniture, cold floors, and bare walls—not exactly comforting. And on a decorative level, textiles offer a great opportunity to express your personal style.

Available in an endless variety of materials, weights, patterns, and textures, the types of textiles you choose, and how you mix them, make a home totally unique.

Communicate with patterns. Express yourself with the scales and types of designs you choose. They can skew playful and modern (say, large-scale geometrics or ethnic and animal prints) or sophisticated and traditional (say, smaller florals, plaids, or stripes).

Mix and match. Be sure to vary the types and scales of the patterns you plan to use, but always include a common color. For visual variety, throw in one small dose of an unexpected hue that's not in any of the patterns.

Don't forget the floor. Rugs are one type of textile that you should never overlook. Whether you go for a patterned Oriental or a solid plush shag, what's underfoot can make a huge difference in the look and feel of a room.

Whichever way your style leans, I believe in dressing a room with layers of textiles and patterns to add warmth, interest, and personality.

• • •

Don't overlook how important textiles and patterns are to a home. A mod motif can suddenly funk up a room, or one special pattern can serve as the element that ties an entire design together. While it's easy to get caught up in the big-ticket furniture purchases, fabric choices will be critical in adding color and texture, and in making your home *you*.

LEFT: The colors for this small Moroccan-style den, which is used as a changing room and occasional play area, were pulled straight from the soft, faded palette of the vintage rug. Lush textures on the ribbed-velvet round-backed chair, piles of colorful pillows on the daybed, and brightly patterned roman shade all contribute to the feeling that you're inside a Bedouin tent.

OPPOSITE: Complete with a princess gown on a dress form and a magic wand, this room channels a storybook vibe. I think every kid (large and small) should have a playful, fantastical element in his or her room to spark imagination and creativity.

Casa Colonial

These clients, a young family, wanted to recognize their Indian heritage while keeping the overall look light, airy, and modern. Since they didn't feel comfortable with color on the walls, we relied on pieces of Asian art and select pops of saturated hues, common in Indian design, to add vibrancy. We also chose mostly solid upholstery for the large pieces, leaving the patterns to accent pillows or a chair in order to keep the look serene and global rather than over-the-top ethnic. Fabrics with lots of texture add dimension and interest to their home.

In the living room, family heirlooms, like the Indian artwork and elephant sculpture in the corner, intermingle with contemporary white sofas.

LEFT: Too much pattern would have competed with the vaulted, beamed ceiling, so instead we played up texture in this media room. With Italian linen on the sofa and storage ottoman, wool-upholstered chairs, and a shag rug, the effect is very tactile and cozy.

BELOW LEFT: In the dining room, reupholstering the chairs in a Craftsman-inspired print better suited the furniture and light fixture. Custom cotton sateen drapes in a rich blue gray instantly made the room feel more elegant.

BELOW RIGHT: This graphic Regency-style fabric, fashioned into drapes, dramatically frames the archway between the family room and living room.

OPPOSITE TOP: Pillows in a modern large-scale floral print and a Chinese coffee table that I had lacquered electric blue add a sophisticated yet playful feel.

OPPOSITE BOTTOM: When walls are left white, anything placed against them will stand out in stark relief, especially this vibrant yellow-velvet headboard. A mix of other textiles—a soft linen duvet, a cut-velvet bench, silk lampshades—in various shades of brown make the room feel layered and cozy. Meanwhile, small doses of interesting pattern, like these mottled, horn-inlaid nightstands and Moorish pillows, help draw the eye to the bed.

LEFT: All the fabrics in this little boy's room have a velvety texture, and many of the cushions piled high on the daybed have more tactile details, like embroidery and quilting, for added interest. We deliberately chose striped fabrics and more subdued colors that didn't scream "kid's room." Form and function were equally important. For example, the storage ottoman and the painted wooden bench both hold toys and double as seating.

BELOW LEFT: Instead of putting Disney characters on the wall, which a child could quickly grow out of, I hung framed vintage photos of old airplanes, images that seem equally appropriate at two or twelve.

BELOW RIGHT: Lined up like toy soldiers in a window, the little boy's stuffed animal collection becomes an attractive display.

OPPOSITE: In the little girl's bathroom, we kept a feminine palette but went more muted. An antique Hamadan rug in a Fair Isle–like pattern helps to counter the large expanses of cold tile and porcelain. Using more sophisticated fabrics, like the cut-velvet window treatments and ribbon-stripe-silk-covered stool, ensures that the girl will grow into the room rather than out of it.

CHAPTER SEVEN

texture

+

layer

No one would ever call me a minimalist.

In fact, I've even adopted the motto "More is more," from the title of a book on Tony Duquette, a renowned decorator who never played it safe. Like him, I tend to push the envelope in my designs with more pattern, more texture, and more accessories. Using a variety of textures in a room gives it dimension. So even if you stick with a monochromatic or neutral color scheme, you can add interest by blending a sleek silk with a soft linen and a nubby jute. Layering is one of the simplest yet most important principles of design. When you layer different elements, whether patterns, textures, or even objects—books, knickknacks, toss cushions— you create character and interest. Think about how much richer your home looks when you decorate an empty table or arrange patterned pillows on a sofa. Those finishing touches help to fill your space, imbuing it with real warmth and your own personal style. There are a few simple things you can do to bring this principle to life in your own home.

Create tablescapes. Dressing up surfaces with a variety of interesting objects instantly adds personality to a room, but it's important to group items in a thoughtful way to avoid a jumbled look. A successful arrangement will have diversity in scale, color, shape, or texture to catch your eye.

Embellish the plain. I find it hard to pass up any opportunity to add ornamentation. Add trimming to window treatments, pillows, lampshades, and other soft goods.

Be touchy-feely. Paint is flat, but wallpaper often has dimension to it. Think about how things feel to the touch, not just how they look. Mix up velvet with bouclé, or sleek metal with rustic wicker. The contrast keeps things interesting.

Layer it on. Accessorize with extra pillows, throws, and more. Even art can be layered: lean framed photos casually against a wall, slightly overlapping one another.

• • •

There are so many ways to add details and dimension to your home; you just have to start experimenting. If you'd normally choose something plain, try to step outside your comfort zone and go for fancy. Create an interesting vignette on your entry table or bookcase. Ignore the part of your brain that automatically says "too busy" when you think about mixing multiple patterns in a room. Take a risk! You can always change it back if it doesn't work.

The contrasting glazed stripes on each dining chair give the linen upholstery a more contemporary edge and echo the deep blue black we chose for the walls. Every dining room should have a bit of drama, and the glossy, black, built-in Hollywood Regency–style cabinet, the Murano chandelier, and the gilt sunburst mirror do the trick here. Layering the rugs—an antique patterned Khotan atop a larger heathered jute rug—creates even more varied texture and helps to foster a less formal vibe.

OPPOSITE: A custom metal console shows off a collection of Etsy and eBay finds.

ABOVE: The bed is a true showstopper in the master suite. Originally, it was covered in beige Ultrasuede, but we reupholstered it with this amazing rug. It has wonderful texture and pattern, and the border of the rug lines up perfectly along the bedrail. Since this piece became such a focal point, we kept the rest of the room understated. Again, the focus was on texture, with a soft jute rug, nubby lampshades, a charcoal-velvet armchair, and neutral grasscloth wallpaper that create a subtle backdrop for the bed.

BELOW: Repeating custom design elements is a no-no in my book, but in this case my client's girlfriend, with whom I've worked on several projects, convinced me otherwise. She had recently sold her house to move in with him and missed the Moroccan stars on her closet doors. We built these wardrobes in the guest room to serve as her dressing area. The suzani bedspread gives this otherwise subdued room a hip spark but can be put away when more conservative guests, like the homeowners' parents, come to visit.

LEFT TOP: Among the tableau of pillows, a bright red suzani catches your eye. These small pops of color break up the monotony. Using a mix of textures, patterns, and colors is key.

LEFT MIDDLE: As a cigar smoker, my client couldn't resist this cool vintage ashtray. We looked for other interesting ones and incorporated them into the decor.

BELOW: Doesn't this screening room feel like a cozy cocoon? That was the goal. We wanted a casual air in here because it leads to the outdoor area, and we chose lots of worn-in fabrics, like the vintage linen on the custom sofa and the French ticking on the pillows. The old wheel coffee table also cultivates the rustic, go-ahead-put-your-feet-up vibe. Heavy jute wallpaper on the ceiling, the last element to go in, ended up making the room. As thick as a rug, it adds interesting texture, highlights the lofty ceiling height, and helps with the acoustics.

RIGHT: Situated between the kitchen and the family room, the breakfast area coordinates in shades of gray. We gave this modern tulip-base table a striped mink marble top for a graphic touch and replaced uncomfortable chairs with supportive and stylish wingbacks. I love how the gray pairs with the rich brown shade of the wide oak-plank flooring.

BELOW: The kitchen had been recently redone and didn't need much tinkering to make it jell with the rest of the house. Repainting the cabinets a sophisticated dark gray brought warmth and character to the room. We swapped out the Carrera marble on the island for dark soapstone to create more of a casually mismatched feel. Vintage-inspired industrial stools were a funky choice that keeps the room from feeling too sleek and modern.

LEFT: A brass-accented sunburst mirror reflects the dining room's chandelier and artwork.

BELOW: An open-air covered terrace feels as sophisticated as the interior of the house. Cool, nautical-inspired metal-and-glass pendants and retro-looking bathing-beauties artwork by Greg Lotus give a nod to the nearby pool. The neutral gray-and-taupe palette gets electrified with pops of blue (the faux-leather wingback chair) and orange (the accent pillow and the piping on the ottomans). Limed-oak tables topped with zinc give this outdoor room a rustic-industrial spin.

OPPOSITE TOP: Deep, dark colors create a dramatic mood in the office. The quirky blue wingback chair gets paired with a once blond, now espresso-colored desk, and both sit atop a simple geometric rug. To keep the room from going too far to the dark side, we wallpapered the backs of the bookcases in a light-colored grasscloth and brought in an overscale drip-glazed lamp in an unexpected jade-green hue.

OPPOSITE BOTTOM: More beach-themed Slim Aarons artwork hangs above the benches outside the pool house.

LEFT: This built-in outdoor kitchen and barbecue area was designed with parties in mind. Comfortable stools, which coordinate with the seating area across the yard, can be pulled up to the Calcutta marble–topped bar while the homeowner mans the grill. And with charming wicker-ball lights adding a magical twinkle at night, the party can keep going into the wee hours.

BELOW: With its classic blue-and-white palette, this outdoor seating area is the epitome of Hamptons chic. We funked up the well-made Summit furniture with a few patterned pillows and added some mink marble–topped chrome side tables to keep it from feeling too matchy-matchy. The X-base furniture was one of the first things we purchased, and I designed a geometric railing to echo that detail. Shrubs and plants, including lemon and kumquat trees, bring in more vivid color.

RIGHT: It can be a challenge to find good-looking (and comfortable) outdoor dining furniture. Rather than settle for one or the other, we picked out regular upholstered chairs and had them outfitted with outdoor foam, re-covered in outdoor fabric, and weather-sealed. While the style is tailored, pale chartreuse-and-taupe stripes tone down any sense of traditionalism. I designed the custom table with a concrete top and an antique metal base.

BELOW LEFT: Outside the cabana, a pair of benches welcomes even those in wet swimsuits. They have a weathered, driftwood-like finish and upholstery that has the washed-out look of watercolors, so you don't have to worry about messing them up.

BELOW RIGHT: Beadcrete, made from tiny reflective beads set into concrete, lines the organically shaped pool, giving it interesting texture and reflectivity.

Venice Beach Craftsman

These clients were decorating their first home, but they wanted a collected-over-time look. We spent a couple of months shopping for special pieces in order to capture this authentic, layered feeling. Paint was also a major factor in transforming their home into a cozier, more Zen space.

When shopping for outdoor furniture, focus on the frames. You can always change the cushions, as we did for this set. New, plusher cushions made with custom fabrics gave the couch and armchairs the chic look we wanted and created a great backdrop for tons of patterned pillows. The bench was an indoor piece the homeowners had planned to give to Goodwill, but its curving lines complemented the rest of the furniture. With a new cushion made of outdoor fabric (matching one of the throw pillows), it gives the seating area a mix-and-match vibe.

A mix of custom cushions brings texture and pattern to the neutral sofa, and slightly battered accessories, such as the record case, antique Ball jars, and luggage, add to the lived-in vibe. Nubby bouclé ottomans and floor pillows made with rich velvet fabrics in 1970s-inspired designs offer extra casual seating for when the couple entertains.

A collection of silvery, soot-blackened decanters adorns the mantel. Cleaning them would have ruined their special patina.

Juxtaposing the industrial to the organic ensures that my interiors don't appear studied and showroom-like. When you get this balance right, the results are effortlessly cool. Vintage oilcans, an old camera, and even a bowling pin are elevated to art when displayed on shelves lined with textured grasscloth.

OPPOSITE: A designer my clients had previously worked with chose the rug, dining table, and chairs, but the coloring didn't quite work. Once the chair legs were refinished to a grayer tone to match the table, there was instant cohesion. Painting two different smoky gray tones on the formerly white walls helped bring together the industrial yet earthy feel the homeowners wanted.

CHAPTER EIGHT

color

+

light

Now that you've seen some of my work,

you've probably noticed I don't shy away from color. It's one of

those little things in life that make me truly happy. When I look

at my deck of paint chips and see all those wonderful, varied

possibilities fanned out before me, I feel giddy and inspired. Color

is essential to design because it's the very first thing you react to

when you walk into a room. It truly sets a mood and affects our

emotions (think about when you "feel blue" or "see red"). Light is

similarly important because it creates ambience and we take our

cues from its intensity. And it's not just the quality of the light but

the type and style of the fixture itself that goes a long way toward

establishing the tone in a space. If you really want to transform

your home, just pick up a paintbrush or install a new light fixture.

It's worth experimenting to get it right.

Hues you can use. Contrary to what most people think, dark colors can make a room feel larger, so don't be afraid of them. Look for sophisticated shades with gray or black bases, which are subtler and more neutral than white-based brights. They'll blend with a variety of hues, which makes them much easier to work with.

Scheme from the start. Always plan the colors for your whole house at once in order to create a cohesive look. In an open-plan house, choose hues that transition naturally from room to room. This strategy also works well in a more traditional layout with defined rooms, or you can go to the other extreme and use unrelated colors to make each room stand on its own.

More is better. You can't hang just one overhead fixture and call it a day. Layer multiple points of light in every room. Table lamps, floor lamps, and sconces all give off flattering, indirect light that reflects off the walls and ceiling to create a more pleasing ambience. (And always use the dimmer switch.)

Make it your own. The style of each fixture should enhance your decor. You can tailor a lamp in so many ways by changing out the shade or adding trim or a new chain. Even the types of bulbs you choose will influence the quality of light. For me, adding shine and a bit of sparkle to a room will never go out of style.

• • •

Color and light go hand in hand, as they both have such a huge effect on our emotions. To get them right, you just have to experiment, and remember that neither represents a lifelong commitment. Don't be afraid to try a bold color on the walls, pick out zany accent pillows, or opt for a funky floor lamp. The hues on your walls can be repainted, you can buy new pillow covers, and you can reconfigure a lamp with new shades or finishes to suit a different room. Changing things up with a fabulous new fixture or a fun accent color will instantly refresh your decor.

LEFT: To brighten up this dark room, we kept the walls light and framed the windows simply with dramatic drapes. Now the sunlight streams in unimpeded. The deep, rich red of the leather wingback chairs and detailed curtains creates contrast, lending this conversation area the air of a sophisticated study.

OPPOSITE: To reduce the dark, heavy feel of the beams, we refinished them to look like driftwood. Classic sofas, reupholstered in an unexpected orange-and-white chevron pattern, suddenly feel fresh and up-to-date. Cutting off the sleeves of the chandelier to expose the bulbs gave it a slight industrial edge.

Artist's Abode

My clients for this project were a couple who have since married. Before we began work, there seemed to be a major disconnect between their traditional ranch and her unconventional tastes. She had an affinity for Mexican religious culture, especially the Day of the Dead, so I set out to interpret the contrast of vivid hues and gothic themes associated with the holiday. She's also an artist, and once she shared her work with me, I was even more inspired to help her express her colorful personality. While she loved vibrant colors like pink and red, her husband was something of a minimalist, and she wanted to create a home that was inclusive of his tastes as well. We struck a balance by using orange throughout the house and keeping most of the furnishings neutral so that the artwork and accessories would stand out. Shopping trips to Olvera Street in LA's Little Mexico turned up crosses, candleholders, and other kitschy artifacts. In the end, every room had the pop of color and interest she craved, but the clean lines made her husband feel at home, too.

The homeowners painted the abstract piece above the bed together, making it especially meaningful to them. We translated its bold color scheme into the room's design by painting the walls orange and dressing the bed in turquoise. A pair of purple Indian chairs, a red trunk, and a candy-striped rug add to the room's vibrant hacienda style.

LEFT: Not many people would think to put an old altarpiece in their guest bedroom, but that's what makes this home so interesting and unique. My client turned it into a secular shrine that showcases her art projects and other random collectibles. Prayer candles add to the ambience.

BELOW: Turquoise foo dogs, used as bookends in the master bedroom, bring color and character to an ordinary shelf.

OPPOSITE: A fake stuffed rooster keeps watch over the dining room from his perch on the buffet. We brought in colorful place settings from Cost Plus World Market and whimsical candelabra from Urban Outfitters for an exuberant tabletop display.

Los Angeles Atelier

A little global, a little glam, and a lot Zen. That describes my client, a hairstylist who manages the coifs of Hollywood A-listers and travels the world for work and pleasure. Mixing an array of ethnic influences, unusual finds, and saturated hues gave his 1930s Spanish colonial home a lighthearted, cosmopolitan vibe that's true to his personal style.

In the cozy family room, vibrant kelly green and orange accents have a big impact. The homeowner had wanted to toss the midcentury modern love seat, but I convinced him it was a keeper and just warmed it up with funky ethnic textiles. Floor pillows made from kilim rugs, a glitzy brass-and-crystal light fixture, and a fluffy flokati rug add to the textured, eclectic mix. And in a nod to Southern kitsch, I hung a framed illustration of old hunting rifles over the sofa.

LEFT: In the dining room, deep charcoal gray on the walls sets a dramatic mood. Vivid sapphire blue chairs and a modern painting bring in needed doses of color. The faux-antler chandelier—a tongue-in-cheek reference to the homeowner's roots in the South, where hunting is a big part of the culture—helps lighten the vibe.

BELOW LEFT: Black furnishings and white accents pop against the deep hunter green walls. It's very masculine yet urbane, which is exactly the look my client wanted. We added another custom shade to this reflective eBay fixture, giving the light that signature golden glow.

BELOW RIGHT: As a hairstylist, the homeowner often has clients drop by for blowouts, so we cleverly hid a styling station right in the family room. The stool and ornate mirror are totally functional—but so decorative that they blend in with the rest of the decor.

RIGHT: Pops of sunny yellow on the chair cushion and a bright ikat pillow punch up the neutral scheme in this room. Adding a black lacquered shade modernized the lamp, a family heirloom. Coating the inside of a shade with gold foil is one of my go-to tricks. The black lacquer causes the light to shine out only from the top and bottom of the shade, and the gold gives off a glowy, warm hue, creating a moody effect.

BELOW LEFT: Outside we went for an ethnic, organic look with a rustic wood-slab table, a Regency couch, and a painterly striped rug.

BELOW RIGHT: With a cove ceiling typical of Spanish colonials, it made sense to continue the blue-gray hue onto the ceiling. The lines of the bookcases and pass-through mimic the ceiling's curve.

Electric Eclectic

This project pushed me outside my comfort zone. My client talks fast, he thinks fast, and he has lots of interests. He needed a house that would stimulate him. When he bought this Los Angeles midcentury home, he asked for my opinion. I told him to scrap the bright orange cabinets and lime green walls. But that was exactly why he had bought it in the first place! He's passionate about color, which isn't surprising considering his Cuban heritage. I tend to do one crazy thing in a room or a house, balancing vibrant and subtle elements. He wanted to do it all outside the box. We were at a standoff because I didn't know if I could go as wild as he wanted. But I learn from my clients. He pushed me, and it made me a better designer. The project brought me back to my younger days, before I was a quote-unquote designer, when it was just fun to decorate with absolute abandon. Together we imagined a big kid's house filled with bold hues and whimsical knickknacks. Visitors can't help but walk in with smiles on their faces because it's just so light and fun—and that's a direct reflection of his personality.

Saturated colors make the cabana a lively gathering spot. A pack of striking papier-mâché animal masks made in Haiti keep watch over the room. At once playful and peculiar, they fit right into the scheme.

ABOVE: In his living room, a slim-striped rug from Paul Smith and whimsical artwork brought in the color he craved. The sofa style stayed true to the midcentury house, but we chose upholstery made from vintage parachute material to give it a hipper edge. Natural, earthy tones, from the coffee table to the bamboo blinds, help ground the look.

RIGHT: Beautiful red proteas and vibrant fruit in a turquoise glazed bowl bring more colorful accents to the room. The old turntable and clarinet are another allusion to his love of music.

ABOVE: My client, an actor by trade but a musician at heart, plays this gorgeous grand piano all the time. To offset its conservative sensibility, we paired it with a funky, cowhide-covered desk chair and a modern globe pendant light.

LEFT: A folksy, three-dimensional bust of a sailor has so much personality it nearly leaps off of the wall.

LEFT: "The brighter, the better" should be this client's motto. He lives for color and has an affinity for urban, contemporary looks. At once edgy and childlike, overscale modern art pops against a vivid green wall and a bright blue jute rug. Nothing matches in here, but the collection of unlike things is part of the appeal.

BELOW LEFT: A primary-color scheme brings energy to the pool house and sauna. Instead of typical soothing, spa-like hues, we woke up the space with vibrant yellow paint, unexpected blue school lockers from eBay, and practical red-plastic flooring that allows water to drain.

BELOW RIGHT: Out by the pool, curvaceous lounge chairs act as perfect foils for the angular lines of this midcentury home's architecture.

RIGHT: Showcasing one of his other great passions, motorcycle helmets and model cars rev up interest on the bookshelves.

BELOW: A midcentury home wouldn't be complete without a classic, chic Eames lounge chair. The large drip-glazed lamp, another essential of that era, sets off the architectural desk.

Relaxed Industrial

This young couple are actors with wicked senses of humor, and their home needed to reflect their fun and irreverent attitudes. As newlyweds setting up their first home, they wanted it to reflect their tastes. Luckily, the pair was on the same page style-wise; both loved a mix that was equal parts modern and vintage. They both enjoy entertaining, so we focused on creating spaces ideal for casual gatherings with friends. Since they are very eco-conscious, we also made an effort to reuse things they already owned and went for green options wherever possible. Adding whimsical touches throughout the home conveyed the edgy, boho look they both adore.

To play up the high, pitched ceiling in the bedroom, we hung a huge lantern fixture. It's out of proportion with the rest of the room, but because it's open and airy, it doesn't overwhelm the space.

Some larger homes have a living room, a great room, and a den—three rooms with essentially the same function. Who says you have to make each one a regular sitting room? Since my clients love to entertain, we transformed the former great room into a modern bar area with a full-size pool table and a 1920s Victorian-style piano. Accessorized with vintage barware, the retro metal bar is Prohibition-era chic.

In the corner, we paired a game table with two chic but comfortable leather armchairs. The artwork, vintage army rifle targets that we had framed, continues the playful rec room look.

RIGHT: Unexpected in a nursery, the orange-and-green color scheme gives the room a modern feel. Custom orange, dotted fabric shades and a chair covered in soft, nubby terry cloth make it cozy, too.

BOTTOM LEFT: This superelegant bath had the bones—classic subway tile, a mosaic floor, and sophisticated fixtures—but lacked that special something. Putting up flocked wallpaper in a moody, tone-on-tone floral print instead of paint lends the room a chic and almost girly gothic vibe.

BOTTOM RIGHT: Vintage finds, like a stamp carousel and an old camera, blend with a mercury glass lamp and modern art on an industrial wood console table. The slightly off-center position of the artwork makes it especially eye-catching.

OPPOSITE TOP: The existing cabinets and finishes in this kitchen were so well done, we just painted the walls a pretty, silvery-purple shade, added simple, inexpensive bar stools, and called it a day.

OPPOSITE BOTTOM: Before, the large, angular furniture gave the appearance of a waiting room. We made it more inviting by bringing in the leather ottoman from another room and adding graphic touches like the zebra rug and drapery panels. Personal accessories—guitars, a telescope, jars on the mantel that were used at the couple's wedding—help round out the space and make it feel lived-in.

Carthay Circle Cottage

It's always a pleasure to work with clients who are open-minded and want to get involved in the design process. This young family has a very artsy and earthy vibe. They are drawn to the outdoors and came to the table with their own ideas of how to incorporate environmentally conscious materials into their home. We found interesting ways to display their family heirlooms and used playful touches throughout the house, in both accessories and color choices. The results reflect the family's open spirit, and because of that, everyone—including the kids, dogs, and guests—feels at home here.

In this cottage-style home, we combined a traditional sleigh bed with contemporary pillows and an oversize ethnic vase. A funky raffia chandelier, with mischievous little monkeys literally swinging from the fixture, adds an offbeat touch.

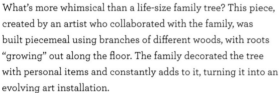

What's more whimsical than a life-size family tree? This piece, created by an artist who collaborated with the family, was built piecemeal using branches of different woods, with roots "growing" out along the floor. The family decorated the tree with personal items and constantly adds to it, turning it into an evolving art installation.

Small bathrooms can be great places to experiment with bold decor. Fun, over-the-top painted stripes were designed to play up the powder room's vintage 1940s lavender-and-yellow tile, which the homeowners had originally wanted to replace. Not only did they save a bundle, but it's now their favorite room in the house.

Clean-lined, neutral furniture offsets more ornate carved-wood pieces, like the Indonesian coffee table and Indian cabinet. With a modern shag rug and a subdued palette, the room embodies the clients' earthy, global tastes.

OPPOSITE: Combining bold colors and interesting patterns imbues this TV room with youthful energy. A mix of teal ombré stripes, an acid-yellow floral pattern, and a print of a phrenology diagram makes it a genuinely fun place to relax and hang out.

CHAPTER TEN

collections

+

kitsch

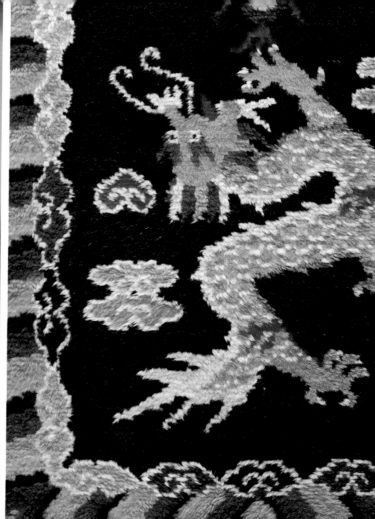

RADJA STAMBOEL
MADE IN SWEDEN

Think about when you visit someone's home

for the first time. You take a look at their bookshelves, the art on the walls, and the tchotchkes on display. It's often these so-called little things that give you the most insight into a person's identity and taste. It's the same when I meet a new client. I glean so much from looking at his or her trinkets and collectibles. In fact, they often end up being the spark that inspires the overall design. That's because everyone, even those who think of themselves as design challenged, gravitates toward certain styles, eras, and colors. We're all like little magpies collecting shiny objects for our nests. Even if it's a vase your grandmother gave you, the fact that you're showing it off in your home means something. That one item—even if it's something I would never in a million years pick out—can end up making the room. I try to help clients discover and express their own taste rather than impose my own, which is why my work is so varied and different. But I still have a strong point of view and a method for making even the wackiest things work. Following a few basic guidelines, and your own instincts, will create successful, inspiring collections.

Lighten up. I like to have fun with design, which is why one of my biggest pet peeves is a stuffy, serious room (think: country clubs, your fussy aunt's house, or anywhere you're afraid to touch things). I want to spend my time in places that have levity and a sense of humor. Not surprisingly, those are qualities I look for in people, too. It's the charming mix of high and low, classy and kitschy, that gives a home personality, and it's why I always bring an element of surprise to my interiors. To achieve that goal, I add something unexpected, whimsical, or downright oddball.

Join the culture club. Do you have a design crush on a certain country or culture? If you're attracted to a region's art, food, or furniture, incorporate some of those items into your decor for a hint of the exotic. Blending cultures creates a sophisticated melting-pot look that I adore, and I don't see anything wrong with displaying a colorful chopstick collection in the kitchen, a grouping of Moroccan lanterns on your back porch, and a Native American rug in the living room. Just avoid going to theme extreme. A few ethnic trinkets look chic and eclectic; a roomful channels "It's a Small World." You don't need a passport full of stamps to pull off this style. Sure, shopping while you travel can't be beat, but if you're short on vacation time and money, just look in the ethnic neighborhoods in your city for inexpensive imports or hit those old standbys: eBay and flea markets.

There's power in numbers. Even the most everyday objects can become a striking display when you group them together. Go big! One or two related objects might catch your eye, but multiples heighten the effect, giving the arrangement weight and power. If you don't want to confine your collection to one particular type of object, like vases, instead choose a theme that you love, say, stars or horses. Then look for them in a variety of media, like statues, paintings, and paperweights.

• • •

Collections can take so many forms, and they speak volumes about their collectors. The art and objects you choose to display can tell the world about your travels, your interests, and your life. Pay attention to the things you are drawn to, whether they are animals or religious artifacts. You may already be collecting and not even have realized it! These are the essentials that personalize your space and truly make a house a home.

LEFT: This carved peacock roosts atop a jewelry box that I found on eBay.

OPPOSITE: In this bedroom, a Mexican headboard cohabits with an ikat-print duvet, Moroccan hanging light fixtures, and French faux-finished nightstands, creating a global vibe.

Beverly Hills Pied-à-Terre

Here's the funny thing about my home: it seems to magically expand to fit whatever new treasure I find. Because I'm constantly out shopping for clients, I often come across items I just have to have for myself. I can't help but collect things I like or think are cool. To me, this means my place is always evolving and I never get bored with my decor. Other people might think I need an intervention. The last time I tried to get my dad to help me pick up a piece of furniture, he refused, saying my place was going to look like an episode of *Hoarders*. Even though he didn't believe me when I told him there was room, I knew exactly where to put it. After a quick-change rearrange, he did come around to my way of thinking. "I don't know how, but now the room looks bigger!" he said. I think it's a testament to the idea that you should always follow your heart when decorating and ignore what other people think. Walking through each room of my home is a little like taking a trip through my favorite countries and design periods. It's a diverse, collected style—one that's thoroughly *me*.

To liven up the all-white kitchen, I brought in pattern with this zigzag-striped runner. Russet-colored drapes and bamboo blinds from Cost Plus World Market coordinate perfectly with the rug. A quirky pineapple chandelier (an eBay find) and a black lacquered dining set from a Chinese antiques shop help make the room feel layered and interesting.

In the living room, I went for an Asian modern vibe with lots of exotic things that remind me of my heritage. A vibrant painted Tibetan cabinet (detail at right), the first "real" piece of furniture I bought, was the catalyst that motivated me to go for a bold color scheme and bring in more Asian style. I went on to mix other influences, such as a very traditional piece—the English secretary—with slightly out-there, hooded canopy chairs. I finished the room with an amazing antique disco ball that I obsessed over for years before finally buying. Together, the effect is glamorous, colorful, dramatic, and fun.

A red stupa (a Buddhist temple jar) and Chinese boxes sit atop a 1970s coffee table, along with a sea of books. No matter how many I have, I can never resist buying more antique volumes at flea markets and thrift shops; the covers and spines can be like works of art in and of themselves.

LEFT: These vintage Indian matchboxes have tremendous detail, like tiny paintings. I keep them in a bowl on my coffee table.

BELOW LEFT: Bright and showy red-lacquered bird figurines make the secretary they're perched on feel much less serious.

BELOW RIGHT: Here, a floor lamp masquerades as a potted gold palm tree. Its graceful fronds ride the line between elegance and kitsch and make it a perfect choice for anyone who has trouble keeping a plant alive.

RIGHT: An Asian figural lamp in the living room doubles as sculpture and adds a pop of color. You don't always need a matching pair of lights if you embrace the mix-and-match feel.

BELOW: Vintage colored-glass bottles line a windowsill in the bathroom. I love how they catch the light.